IMAGES
of America

THE COAST GUARD
IN SAN DIEGO

Pictured are two MH-60 Jayhawk helicopters in the hangar with the American flag in memory of September 11, 2001 (taken September 11, 2008). In response to the terrorist attacks of September 11, 2001, the Coast Guard took actions to create the largest port-security operation since World War II. Coast Guard cutters and aircraft were diverted from more distant operating areas to patrol U.S. ports and coastal waters, and many new policies were created. (Courtesy of PA3 Henry Dunphy.)

ON THE COVER: An HH-65 flies over the Coast Guard command housing located at Point Loma Lighthouse. This iconic San Diego landmark has been owned and operated by the Coast Guard since 1891. The housing was used during the filming of the movie *Top Gun*. (Courtesy Coast Guard Public Affairs.)

IMAGES
of America

THE COAST GUARD
IN SAN DIEGO

Coast Guard Sector San Diego

ARCADIA
PUBLISHING

Copyright © 2010 by Coast Guard Sector San Diego
ISBN 978-0-7385-8014-2

Published by Arcadia Publishing
Charleston SC, Chicago IL, Portsmouth NH, San Francisco CA

Printed in the United States of America

Library of Congress Control Number: 2009935200

For all general information contact Arcadia Publishing at:
Telephone 843-853-2070
Fax 843-853-0044
E-mail sales@arcadiapublishing.com
For customer service and orders:
Toll-Free 1-888-313-2665

Visit us on the Internet at www.arcadiapublishing.com

*This book is dedicated to the men and women of
Coast Guard Sector San Diego, past, present, and future.*

CONTENTS

ACKNOWLEDGMENTS

This book has been no small undertaking, and it has taken a team of people to get it to this point. The authors would like to thank the staff of the Public Affairs Detachment San Diego for their outstanding moral and technical support throughout. Special thanks are due to Captain "Bear" Moseley and the Coast Guard Aviation Association for their guidance, assistance, and resources.

Thank you to the following for their input, whether it came from writing or providing photographs: Dr. David Rosen, Gary and Amy Strebe, the Marini family, Dana Goward, Ed Prink, Bob Hallberg, Stuart Prinkley, Capt. Ken Franke, LCDR Michael Dolan, Comdr. Leon-Geurrero, BMC Hall Grimmett, CWO Carter Owens, and AETC Adam Morton. To the Command Cadre of Sector San Diego, thank you for your support of this project and allowing us to put this book together. LCDR Michael Frawley deserves mention for his initiative in getting the project rolling and getting command approval. Finally, thank you to our editor, Debbie Seracini, for her patience and guidance throughout this process.

All images used in this book come from Coast Guard records, unless otherwise noted.

INTRODUCTION

On December 11, 1935, negotiations between the City of San Diego and the U.S. Government were concluded, which provided 23 acres of tideland for the construction of a Coast Guard air station adjacent to Lindbergh Field, the municipal airport. This project had the strong support of many people and agencies, particularly the Harbor Commission and Department of San Diego and the Chamber of Commerce. The area for this station was deeded to the Coast Guard at no cost, after approval by citizens of San Diego at a municipal election held in April 1935.

Construction of the air station was undertaken in 1936 with funds provided by the Federal Public Works Administration. The M. H. Golden Company, a San Diego building company established in 1927, was the contractor. The area had to be dredged from the bay and filled and brought up to grade level. Long piles were driven into the soil at the building sites for stabilization. The contract called for one hangar with a lean-to, a mess hall, a barracks building, two aprons, a runway to the field, and a small wooden seaplane ramp.

During this time, the Coast Guard continued to maintain an air detachment at Lindbergh Field. The detachment had been established on May 4, 1934, and the first commanding officer was Comdr. Luke Christopher. The detachment operated out of one half of a commercial hangar and Lindbergh Field and was primarily responsible for seeking drug smugglers along the maritime border. On May 21, 1935, Commander Christopher was relieved by Comdr. Elmer F. Stone, one of the most colorful figures of Coast Guard aviation. Commander Stone had been the Coast Guard's first winged naval aviator in 1917. During his illustrious career, Commander Stone had been the pilot in command on the first transatlantic flight in 1919, had worked with the navy to develop carrier operations in the 1920s, and set the then world speed record for seaplanes in 1934. The air detachment would be Commander Stone's last assignment, as he died of a heart attack while on the flight ramp in 1936, shortly before the air station was commissioned.

In April 1937, the air station was commissioned and the air detachment moved across the street onto the newly built grounds. The first commanding officer was Lt. Stanley C. Linholm, who later became commander of the Eleventh Coast Guard District. At the time of its establishment, the air station was the only Coast Guard air base in California.

Coast Guard Air Station San Diego saw no radical changes as a result of the declaration of war in 1941. The unit continued to watch and report the activities of fishing boats in the area, to provide assistance in cases of distress, and to provide transportation by air for other government departments. From October 1943, the air station was designated as an Air Sea Rescue Squadron after the formation of the Air Sea Rescue Agency under the auspices of the Coast Guard. Between January 1, 1944, and December 31, 1944, a total of 124 aircraft went down in the air station's area of responsibility, and of the 201 pilots and crewmen involved 137 were saved.

The Air Sea Rescue Agency was disbanded soon after the war, but the air station continued its search and rescue capabilities, which were enhanced by the continued adoption of helicopters and the use of flying boats and amphibious aircraft.

In August 1944, the commander-in-chief of the U.S. Navy directed Naval Sea Frontier Commanders and Air Force Commands to establish centralized control for Air Sea Rescue operations. In the same month, army authorities established emergency rescue organizations at strategic points, particularly in Alaska and along Air Transport Command routes.

The chief of naval operations further directed that, for the duration of the war, control of Air Sea Rescue be effected through and an integral part of the existing sea-frontier facilities. Required operational units were to be supplied primarily by the Coast Guard. Rescue task units were established consisting of specially equipped and manned air and surface rescue craft under the operational control of the commandants of the various naval districts within the Sea Frontiers. Coast Guard officers were assigned to the Sea Frontier staffs. Operational procedures and communication doctrine were established. The commanding officers of the nine major Coast Guard air stations, San Diego included, were assigned as primary unit commanders. The Coast Guard was to provide search and rescue services, and an Office of Air Sea Rescue was formed at Coast Guard Headquarters in Washington, D.C. to provide support for the operations.

San Diego continued to be in the heart of Coast Guard aviation when, in April 1949, a Coast Guard H03S-1 helicopter, piloted by then Lt. Steward Graham, completed the longest unescorted helicopter flight in the world to that date. The flight was also the first unescorted transcontinental flight by a Coast Guard helicopter. The trip from Elizabeth City, North Carolina, to Port Angeles, Washington, by way of Coast Guard Air Station San Diego, covered a distance of 3,750 miles and took 10.5 days to complete.

The 1940s had seen the Coast Guard champion the development of the use of the helicopter for search and rescue. Coast Guard aviator Frank Erickson, who flew the first rescue mission with a helicopter in 1944, was instrumental in the acceptance of the helicopter for Coast Guard missions. At the same time there were aviators who favored the seaplane for search and rescue efforts. One such aviator was Capt. Donald B. MacDiarmid, who assumed command of Air Station San Diego in 1950 after a distinguished World War II career. While in San Diego, he worked with station personnel to develop open-ocean crash techniques that are still in use by commercial airlines today. Eventually, even Captain MacDiarmid had to accept the helicopter as it replaced the seaplane all together in 1960.

The 1960s saw the expansion of the Coast Guard's responsibilities, with a small rescue boat station operating out of Shelter Island. The base was referred to as Group San Diego during this period, a reflection of the multiple units, both operational and support, that were present. In 1974, the marine safety office was commissioned with a new building on the base, bringing the officer in charge of marine inspections and captain of the port authorities with it.

The arrival of the HH-65 Dolphin and the HU-25 Falcon in the 1980s continued the air station's tradition of housing fixed wing and rotary wing assets. In 1986, the small boat rescue station was moved from Shelter Island to the base, and in 1994, it was commissioned as Small Boat Station San Diego. With the increasing number of units in San Diego receiving support from the administration branch of the base, the base was designated Activities San Diego in the 1980s, a designation it would keep until 2004.

The 1990s saw the arrival of the HH-60J Jayhawk, and for the first time, the air station had only a rotary wing presence, as the Falcons were relocated and the Dolphins replaced by the Jayhawk. With the terrorist attacks of September 11, 2001, the Coast Guard's emphasis on homeland security was increased. Shortly after the Coast Guard moved to the Department of Homeland Security, the name of the base was once again changed, this time to Sector San Diego, in 2004.

As a Sector, the base now houses the air station, the small boat station, all marine safety and inspection functions, and several patrol boats as well as supports multiple tenant commands in the San Diego area.

Today the men and woman stationed at Sector San Diego continue to carry out the Coast Guard missions and work with our Department of Homeland Security brethren to keep our maritime domain safe and secure.

One

Wings and Rotors
Aircraft of San Diego

Since the birth of aviation, the use of aircraft as a means of rescue has been explored. Over the years the Coast Guard has been at the forefront for developing the techniques and procedures for both fixed-wing and rotary-wing rescues at sea. During the 1940s, it was the Coast Guard who championed and developed procedures for the use of helicopters for at-sea rescues. Through the years the Coast Guard has used many different types of aircraft to accomplish a variety of missions, and Air Station San Diego has seen its fair share. From the early seaplanes to the legendary Sikorsky SH-52A helicopter to the modern Sikorsky HH-60J, these aircraft have all played a role in San Diego Coast Guard history.

The RD-4 Dolphin was one of the original aircraft stationed in San Diego. They were acquired by the Coast Guard from 1931 to 1935. Its top speed was 147 mph, it carried a crew of three, and it had a purchase price of $60,000. The RD-4 was the third revision of the aircraft. Its predecessors were all named after stars—Procyon, Adhara, and Sirius. The *Adhara* and *Sirius* were amphibian aircraft, and the *Procyon* was converted at a later date. The Douglas RD started as the *Sinbad*; however, it was lighter and smaller than the Dolphin. The RD-1 through the RD-4 were all completely different as well. They were primarily used for search and rescue and as flying lifeboats. In World War II it was assigned to security patrols along the U.S. coast when the Coast Guard fell under the Department of the Navy.

The JF-2 Duck (small aircraft in center) was one of the first aircraft stationed in San Diego. The search and rescue mission continued to grow, and San Diego was the only air station on the west coast at that time. On a regular basis the JF-2 would deploy to Oakland, California, as a subunit at the Naval Reserve Base. From there it effectively performed search and rescue operations in the San Francisco Bay area.

The JF-2s served ashore at air stations and were carried on board Coast Guard cutters designed to carry aircraft. They were utilized on Bering Sea patrols and on board cutters participating in the Greenland Patrol. Elmer Stone, the second commanding officer of the San Diego Air Detachment, took advantage of the amphibian's excellent performance to establish new world records for amphibians. The JF-2 had a range of 759 nautical miles.

Hall PH-2 patrol plane was the third aircraft stationed in San Diego. This type of amphibian aircraft was originally developed for the navy as a patrol aircraft. The upgraded flying boats purchased by the Coast Guard had more powerful engines as well as more specialized equipment and capabilities for search and rescue duties than the earlier navy models and were therefore given the designation PH-2. They were long-range aircraft capable of operating up to 1,000 miles from base and taking off and landing in rough seas. They were also the largest aircraft ever acquired by the Coast Guard to that time. With the declaration of war in 1941, unit aircraft commenced anti-submarine patrols, but the threat of Japanese submarines off the Pacific Coast proved to be minimal. The unit continued to watch and report the activities of vessels in the area, to provide assistance in cases of distress, and to provide transportation by air for other government departments.

The U.S. Navy Curtiss flying boat NC-4 is seen arriving in the harbor of Lisbon, Portugal, on May 28, 1919. Commander Stone was the pilot and navigator during the flight that originated from a naval air station in Rockaway, New York, on May 8, 1919. The transatlantic flight was the first of its kind and resulted in Commander Stone receiving, among other awards, the Navy Cross.

THE COAST GUARD, at San Diego Air Station, fuels one of the giant Consolidated four-engine patrol bombers now being built for Great Britain. These planes, known as PBY-2Y's are the larg-est and most powerful airplanes in naval service. Production these planes is being stepped up to an amazing pace but maisecrecy is maintained regarding actual delivery to Britain.

This image was scanned from the June 1941 issue of the *Coast Guard Magazine*. The caption reads, "The Coast Guard, at San Diego Air Station, fuels one of the giant consolidated four-engine patrol bombers now being built for Great Britain. These planes, known as PBY-2Ys are the largest and most powerful airplanes in naval service."

Rescue 1, a PBY-5A, was the first aircraft assigned to the Air Sea Rescue Squadron at Coast Guard Air Station San Diego. The squadron was formed in 1943, when the chief of the navy directed Naval Sea Frontier Commanders to establish centralized control for operations. When a distress was reported, a determination of available assets was made. If a search was required, rescue craft were launched. The primary reason for this implementation was the increasing number of offshore crashes, mostly by student pilots. These were the result of the rapid expansion of military aviation during the war. Initially, the amphibious PBY-5A and high-speed rescue craft were chosen as the rescue vehicles, and additional squadrons were formed. In December 1944, the Office of Air Sea Rescue was established at Coast Guard Headquarters. By 1945, Air Sea Rescue was responsible for 165 aircraft and 9 air stations. During that year it had responded to 686 plane crashes. The PBY-5As were replaced by Martin PBM-5Gs following the war.

A PBY-5A with Air Rescue markings is shown sitting on the ramp in San Diego. Nine PBY-5A Catalinas were provided to Coast Guard Air Sea Rescue Squadron 1 in 1943 under the command of Comdr. Chester R. Bender. From October 1943, the air station was designated as an Air Sea Rescue Squadron after the formation of the Air Sea Rescue Agency under the auspices of the Coast Guard. Between January 1, 1944, and December 31, 1944, a total of 124 aircraft went down in waters covered by this unit. Of the 201 pilots and crewmen involved, 137 were saved, 59 were killed outright by mid-air collisions or impact with the water, 2 were missing, and 3 who might have been saved were lost because of improper equipment or the failure to locate them promptly. The Air Sea Rescue Agency was disbanded soon after the war, but the station continued its SAR capabilities that were enhanced by the continued adoption of helicopters and the use of flying boats and amphibious aircraft.

A Martin PBM-3/5 Mariner is seen landing at Air Station San Diego in 1944. There were three Mariners stationed in San Diego in 1944. These aircraft were the backbone of Coast Guard long-range aerial search and rescue efforts in the early postwar years. The very last Mariner model to be produced was the PBM-5A, which was fitted with tricycle landing gear for amphibious operation. It had a range of 3,488 miles.

The Grumman JF-4 was first purchased by the Coast Guard in 1941. It had a hatch on top of the fuselage, just behind the wing, for loading stretchers. Also, a wing rack was added to each aircraft beneath the starboard wing. These racks could hold a depth charge, a bomb, a raft, or search and rescue gear. Many JF-4s were assigned to coastal anti-submarine patrols like the one pictured here.

Pictured is a Grumman JRF-5G Goose painted in World War II gray. The Coast Guard purchased 24 of this model beginning in 1941. They were stationed in San Diego from 1941–1954, and they remained in service until 1954. During World War II they conducted search and rescue, submarine hunting, and troop and supply transportation.

The Douglas R5D-3/4 Skymaster was used from 1945 to 1962. The Coast Guard acquired 15 of these aircraft. Nine were acquired from the navy and the other six from the Air Force. They were used for transport duties, logistical support, search and rescue, duty with the international ice patrol, electronic tests, and photographic mapping flights.

Pictured is a Coast Guard H03S-1 helicopter on the San Diego ramp. In April 1949, a H03S-1 helicopter, piloted by then Lt. Steward Graham, completed the longest unescorted helicopter flight in the world to that date. The flight was also the first unescorted transcontinental flight by a Coast Guard helicopter. The trip from Elizabeth City, North Carolina, to Port Angeles, Washington, by way of Coast Guard Air Station San Diego, a distance of 3,750 miles, took 10.5 days to complete and involved a total flight time of 57.6 hours. The H03S-1 helicopter was built by Sikorsky and used by the U.S Army, Air Force, Navy, and Coast Guard. In the Coast Guard it was primarily used as a search and rescue platform. It had a maximum speed of 78 knots, a cruising speed of 61 knots, and a range of 244 miles.

Three HU-16 Albatross aircraft and a HUS-1G Seahorse helicopter sit on the Coast Guard Ramp at Air Station San Diego in the early 1960s. Both aircraft were used for search and rescue. Both the HUS-1G and HU-16 were acquired by the Coast Guard in 1959. The last HU-16 retired from service in 1983, and the Coast Guard elected not to purchase any new HUS-1Gs when the HH-52s became available.

A HH-3F Pelican, which first entered service in 1969, flies over Harbor Drive with the air station in the background. The HH-3F, manufactured by Sikorsky, was equipped with a single main rotor, twin engines, fully retractable landing gear, and an aft cargo ramp that could be opened in any phase of flight and had the ability to land in the water.

Seven HH-3F Pelicans, a mix of San Diego and Astoria assets, sit on the helicopter ramp awaiting a mission. The HH-3F helicopter began its service in the Coast Guard in January 1969. They were capable of 142 knots with a max range of 620 nautical miles. The Pelican had search radar in the nose and the capability to make water landings.

A HH-3F Pelican is conducting boat-hoist training with a Coast Guard small boat. The Pelican's hoist was capable of lifting 600 pounds with a maximum of 240 feet of useable cable. Pilots and crew are required to maintain proficiency in all missions, but a special emphasis is placed on boat hoisting and rescue swimmer operations to the water.

The HH-52A Seaguard was designed by Sikorsky to land and take off from the water. Here the HH-52A crew is practicing lowering their rescue litter (used for patients who are immobile or have a possible spinal injury) to a Coast Guard 41-foot utility boat. The 41-foot utility boat is still in service today.

A Sikorsky HH-52A crew performs rescue drills off the coast of San Diego in the early 1970s. The HH-52A, known as the Seaguard, came into Coast Guard service in 1963 and was retired from service in 1989. A Coast Guard HH-52A is on display at the Naval Aviation Museum in Pensacola, Florida.

The HH-52H, with over 15,000 lives saved in its 25 years of service, has the honor of having rescued more persons than any other helicopter in the world. This little helicopter, a unique assemblage of proven parts comfortably behind the cutting edge, performed astounding feats in thousands upon thousands of occasions. It became the international icon for rescue and proved the worth of the helicopter many times over.

A Coast Guard HH-52A from San Diego is loaded into the back of a Coast Guard C-130. All rotor blades must be removed to load the HH-52H in the back of the C-130. The C-130s maximum weight is 175,000 pounds with an empty weight of 80,000 pounds, and it can carry up to 65,000 pounds of gas.

A C-130 sits on the San Diego Coast Guard ramp. It has been in service longer than any other aircraft in history. The first one came out in 1955, and other than avionics upgrades, there have only been minor structural changes. It is known as the "work horse" of any service due to its service life, reliability, and ability to lift things. It can fly with two engines out, even if both are on the same side, and it is permitted to shutdown one or two engines in order to prolong endurance. It is designed to land and takeoff on very short fields and was even considered and tested for landing on carriers. They successfully landed it multiple times on a carrier but deemed the operation unsafe.

A Lockheed HC-130 Hercules is seen on the Coast Guard ramp in San Diego. It has four Allison T56-A15 Turboprop engines and a maximum gross weight of 175,000 pounds. The nearest C-130s are stationed in Air Station Sacramento and provide air cover when helicopters are conducting search and rescue cases more than 150 miles offshore. Air cover consists of a radio guard, monitoring weather, and coordinating with shoreside facilities.

Two HU-25 Falcon Guardians fly in formation off the La Jolla. The Falcon was based in San Diego from 1982 to 1996. The Falcons provided the Coast Guard with an aircraft that could arrive on scene quickly and coordinate rescue efforts. Its advanced radar and sensor system was also used extensively to combat drug smugglers.

Members of the Air Station pose on the ramp in front of an HH-65 Dolphin and HU-25 Falcon in 1994. Longtime residents of San Diego may remember seeing the Falcon being towed across Harbor Drive to Lindbergh Field. Since the air station only has a helicopter pad, whenever the Falcon needed to launch, it was towed across to Lindbergh to use the runway. (Courtesy Mario Marini.)

A HH-65B Dolphin is shown on a regular patrol over La Jolla, California, on June 1, 1996. The HH-65B is known for its Fenestron tail. Its purpose is to counteract the torque of the main rotor, like any other tail rotor on a helicopter. However, it sounds quieter than a conventional tail rotor due to the blades' variable angular spacing so that the noise is distributed over different frequencies.

The CG6502, a HH-65A, conducts rescue training with downtown San Diego in the background. Manufactured by Aerospatiale and known as the Dolphin, the HH-65 served in San Diego from 1985 to 1996. A very versatile helicopter capable of operating off the flight deck of Coast Guard cutters, there are more Dolphins in Coast Guard service than any other aircraft.

A HH-60 Jayhawk and HH-65 Dolphin fly in formation over the San Diego Convention Center in the late 1990s. The HH-65 was visiting from Air Station Los Angeles, located at the Los Angeles International Airport. Sector San Diego and Air Station Los Angeles cover each other's search and rescue responsibilities when one station's assets are in maintenance.

Two MH-60 Jayhawk helicopters from Coast Guard Sector San Diego conduct a flyover of the San Diego Chargers stadium for Military Appreciation Day on September 1, 2005. The Chargers show their support for the military every year with a flag-folding ceremony, color guard presentation, and awards ceremony honoring outstanding achievements made by military members.

Under a full moon and with downtown San Diego in the background, Coast Guard HH-60J 6025 prepares to take off from the ramp for a night mission. The Coast Guard motto, *Semper Paratus* ("Always Ready"), means that there are no "after hours" for crews. The Sector San Diego Coasties stand ready to respond 24 hours a day, seven days a week, 365 days a year.

Operation Thin Mint 2009 occurred when 184,108 boxes of Thin Mint cookies were sent to deployed U.S. Troops. An MH-60 Jayhawk from Sector San Diego picked up the cookies from the USS Midway Museum to symbolize their send-off to the troops. Over 1,800 Girl Scouts and San Diegans participated in the event.

Flight mechanic Andy Famula works with ground crewman Steven Conrad to hook up a pallet of Girl Scout Thin Mint cookies. The cookies, located on the deck of the USS Midway Museum on the Embarcadero, were airlifted as a part of a ceremony in which the Girl Scouts send all the cookies they sold to troops overseas.

A HH-60J Jayhawk lowers a battery down to the Aids to Navigation Team San Diego on the south jetty of the entrance to Mission Bay. Even when performing simple missions, such as delivering a battery, Coast Guard units work together to support one another as demonstrated by the air station delivering the battery and the small boat station delivering the personnel to the jetty (background).

Preparing to depart on a mission, a HH-60J Jayhawk spins up on the ramp outside of maintenance control. The HH-60J, continuing a long line of Sikorsky Coast Guard aircraft, has served in San Diego since 1996. A very dependable aircraft, the Jayhawk is an excellent search and rescue platform with the capability to go 300 miles offshore, search for 45 minutes, conduct a rescue, and return to home base.

The Coast Guard Jet, C-37A Gulfstream V, taxied across North Harbor Drive from Lindbergh Field to Coast Guard Sector San Diego in early 2009. The Gulfstream is stationed in Air Station Washington and is assigned to carry out the mission of providing worldwide command and controlling air transportation for the secretary of Homeland Security, the commandant of the Coast Guard, and other personnel authorized by the commandant.

A MH-60J Jayhawk performs search-and-rescue demonstrations for distinguished visitors at Coast Guard Sector San Diego. In the background is Naval Air Station North Island. The rescue swimmer is lowered down the hoist hook by the flight mechanic controlling the hydraulic rescue hoist. The flight mechanic will also provide directional commands to guide the pilot into the correct position to make a successful hoist.

Two

Oars to Props
Boats and Cutters of San Diego

The Coast Guard is the nation's oldest continuous seagoing service, having been established in 1790 as the Revenue Cutter Service. The Coast Guard has a long, proud history of search and rescue that has long been done without the use of aircraft. From lifeboats propelled by manpower to propeller-driven craft, the development and use of seagoing vessels has been an integral part of the Coast Guard and San Diego. Today modern "cutters," vessels in length of 65 feet or more with crew living spaces, patrol the bay, coast, and maritime borders, working with the smaller utility and response boats from Small Boat Station San Diego, to perform a wide array of Coast Guard missions.

U.S.S. GLENDALE PF-36

The USS *Glendale* (PF-36), a Tacoma-class frigate, was commissioned on October 1, 1943. The ship sailed from San Diego in January 1944 under command of Lt. Comdr. Harold J. Doebler of the U.S. Coast Guard. Her missions in World War II were anti-submarine and anti-aircraft escort of merchant ships. The Coast Guard manned and operated close to 70 of these ships.

The Coast Guard cutter *Wachusett* is a 255-foot, Owasco class, high-endurance cutter. She was commissioned out of San Pedro, California, in 1946 and did her sea trials off the coast of Southern California, including San Diego. The *Wachusett* would call Port Angeles, Washington, her homeport and served in Vietnam from 1968 to 1969.

The Coast Guard cutter *Androscoggin* is shown alongside the navy transport vessel USS *Fuller* off the coast of Southern California in the late 1940s. The *Androscoggin*, a 255-foot-high endurance cutter, was built and commissioned out of San Pedro, California. She would later be used in the Paramount motion picture *Assault on a Queen* in 1966.

The 40-foot steel utility boat was used in the Coast Guard from the 1950s to early 1970s. It took the place of the wooden picket boat and was later replaced by the 41-foot utility boat. Here it is pictured in the San Diego Harbor with Naval Air Station North Island in the background.

The Coast Guard cutter *Eagle* motors next to the *Cape Jellison*, a 95-foot patrol boat in 1965. The *Eagle* sails all over the world training cadets from the Coast Guard Academy and candidates from Officer Candidates School on basic seamanship and navigation. It has a full-time crew of 6 officers and 56 enlisted in addition to the 150 cadets that it can carry.

Pictured is the WPB-95317B *Cape Jellison* in the San Diego Bay in 1965. It is a 95-foot Cape Class patrol boat fitted for search and rescue with scramble nets, a towing bit, and a large searchlight. It was built in the Coast Guard Yard in Curtis Bay, Maryland, in 1955. The Island Class, 110-foot patrol boat replaced the Cape Class in the late 1980s.

The Coast Guard cutter *Eagle* was built in 1936 and used as a training vessel for German naval cadets. It was commissioned as *Horst Wessel* and following World War II was taken as a war prize by the United States. In 1946, the barque was commissioned into Coast Guard service as the *Eagle* and sailed from Bremerhaven, Germany, to New London, Connecticut. It is pictured off the San Diego coast in July 1965.

Coast Guard cutter *Androscoggin* stopped in San Diego on its way back from Vietnam. The crew was cited for exceptionally meritorious service from January 1, 1967, to March 31, 1968, in connection with the interdiction of enemy forces and supplies into Vietnam. They maintained a close vigil over 1,200 miles of coastline and more than 50,000 licensed watercraft and created one of the most effective coastal barriers in naval history.

The Coast Guard cutter *Flagstaff* is seen off the San Diego coast in late 1974. She was loaned by the navy to the Coast Guard for evaluation as an option for replacing the aging 95-foot cutter. The Coast Guard's interest in the craft was its speed and ability to interdict smugglers and other suspicious craft approaching the U.S. coast. She operated out of San Diego and other Californian ports during the Coast Guard's evaluation.

Pictured is the WPB 82377 *Point Hobart* in the late 1970s. It was stationed in Oceanside, California, and routinely patrolled the waters around San Diego. During the Nixon presidency, she, in concert with the patrol boat *Point Divide*, performed Presidential Support Duty. They took turns patrolling off the coast in the security zone around the president's retreat for three days before being relieved by the other cutter.

The Coast Guard 41-foot utility boat (UTB) is pictured off the San Diego Coast in the 1980s. The 41-foot UTB is still used today. They were originally built in 1974 for a purchase price of $156,000. Today it is used for search and rescue, maritime law enforcement, marine environmental protection, and recreational boating safety.

The *Californian* was built in 1983–1984 at Spanish Landing in San Diego Bay by the Nautical Heritage Society, with permission from the Port of San Diego. The image is from 1984 when the *Californian* was first launched, or christened. *The Californian* launched from the Coast Guard Base, as a previously planned *Californian* launching was aborted at Spanish Landing due to the trailer sinking into the launch mud.

The Coast Guard cutter *Venturous*, a 210-foot, medium-endurance cutter, is performing helicopter in-flight refueling with a San Diego–based H-3. The *Venturous*, commissioned in 1968 in Baltimore, Maryland, called San Diego its homeport for several years between 1968 and 1994. The *Venturous* was involved in several high-profile search-and-rescue cases off the coast of Mexico during her time in San Diego.

A HH-65 Dolphin approaches for landing on the flight deck of the Coast Guard cutter *Venturous*. The HH-65 is capable of landing and operating from the flight deck of all Coast Guard cutters; a capability that the HH-60 Jayhawk does not have. When cutters deploy for a long patrol, they will often have an aircrew and helicopter attached for the duration.

The Coast Guard cutter *Venturous* crew is ready on the flight deck for an incoming helicopter to do in-flight refueling. Note the fuel hose laid out on the deck while the ground crew waits. The landing signal officer (in white) is responsible for guiding the helicopter in. A navy aircraft carrier is in the background.

A San Diego–based HH-3 spins on the deck of the Coast Guard cutter *Jarvis*. The *Jarvis*, a 378-foot, high-endurance cutter based out of Hawaii, was commissioned in 1971. This photograph was most likely taken while the Jarvis was in the Southern California area and was taking advantage of the San Diego–based helicopters to conduct proficiency training.

A 25-foot Defender Class boat opens up the throttle while on patrol in San Diego Bay. The Defender Class boats were developed in response to the September 11, 2001, attacks and are used by Maritime Safety and Security Teams (MSST), Maritime Security Response Team (MSRT), and Marine Safety Units (MSU). Powered by two outboard engines, the Defender Class excels at high-speed maneuvers.

The Coast Guard Auxiliary participates in a parade along Harbor Drive in San Diego. Pictured is an Aids to Navigation boat with a special appearance by the Safe T Seal. The Coast Guard Auxiliary is a volunteer organization for the Coast Guard specializing in recreational boating safety. Today there are over 600 members assisting Sector San Diego.

Pictured are an Aids to Navigation servicing boat, two rescue boats, two 41-foot utility boats, an 87-foot patrol boat, and two 110-foot patrol boats in the San Diego Bay in 2003. These boats patrol the Coast Guard's San Diego area of responsibility stretching from the Mexican border to the San Onofre Power Plant and out to 200 nautical miles.

San Diego Coast Guard Maritime Security and Safety Team conduct a sweep of a possible target of interest during a training exercise. The security teams were created after September 11, 2001, to specialize in protecting local maritime assets against terrorism and constantly run through possible scenarios for training. This training is often conducted in conjunction with other Coast Guard assets, such as small boats or helicopters.

The photographs show Coast Guard Aids to Navigation Team San Diego working buoys in San Diego Bay. The Aids to Navigation Team is responsible for maintaining the navigation aids in the channel. This involves regularly inspecting them to make sure they are in the proper location, that the light and sound signals are indicating correctly, and that the concrete block (known as the sinker) and chain that holds it in place is in good condition. The responsibility for maintaining the aids fell with the lighthouse tenders located on Ballast Point until 1939, when it was then turned over to the Coast Guard base. The Aids to Navigation Team consists of six to seven personnel and one 21-foot boat.

The Coast Guard cutter *George Cobb*, a 175-foot buoy tender, is home-ported out of San Pedro, California. The *George Cobb* is responsible for maintaining Aids to Navigation on the Southern California coast and makes regular trips down to San Diego to attend to aids too large for the local Aids to Navigation unit. Here the *George Cobb* is seen participating in a vertical insertion exercise with two HH-60 Jayhawks.

A Coast Guard Maritime Security and Safety Team 25-foot response boat escorts a U.S. Navy nuclear submarine out of San Diego Bay. The Coast Guard works closely with the navy to enforce security zones around high-value assets such as submarines and carriers throughout the San Diego area. A navy frigate is inbound in the background.

Members of San Diego Maritime Security and Safety Team are delivered by an Air Station San Diego HH-60J to a vessel of interest during a training exercise. This method of delivery, also known as vertical insertion, allows the boarding team to quickly deploy to the deck of a vessel and secure an area. The helicopter can then back off and provide cover for the boarding team from the air.

Crewmembers of the Coast Guard cutter *Edisto*, a 110-foot patrol boat, score a direct hit during a gunnery exercise. The *Edisto*, the 13th Island Class patrol boat, was commissioned on January 7, 1987. It carries a crew of 16 and spends a lot of time patrolling the international waters off of Mexico looking for drug smugglers.

Coast Guard 25439, a 25-foot response boat, patrols San Diego Bay with the USS Midway in the background. San Diego boat crews constantly patrol the bay enforcing security zones, looking out for safety violations or security threats. San Diego bay has a very large naval presence and coordination between the navy and Coast Guard is important to making sure those assets are safe.

Members of San Diego's Maritime Safety and Security Team practice fast-roping to the deck over the Coast Guard ramp with downtown San Diego in the background. This method of deployment, also known as vertical insertion, requires coordination between the pilots up front, the flight mechanic in the back, and the crewmembers going out the door.

Coast Guard cutter *Bertolf* (WMSL 750), the flagship of the National Security Cutters (NSC), was christened on November 11, 2006. She conducted sea trials off the coast of San Diego with crews from Sector San Diego in early 2009. She has capabilities matched to maritime security and national defense mission requirements. The NSC has a stern ramp to accommodate small-boat launch and recovery in higher sea states than legacy cutters.

Crewmembers from Regional Dive Locker West prepare to dive underwater to inspect the hull of the Coast Guard cutter *Sea Otter*, home-ported in San Diego on October 20, 2008. The Coast Guard recently created regional dive lockers and teams on both coasts capable of responding to apportioned or emergent operations.

PO1 Mike Boyle and Dusty, a K-9 explosives detection team from Marine Safety and Security Team Los Angeles, are hoisted in a basket from an MH-60 Jayhawk helicopter during vertical insertion training in San Diego Bay September 24, 2008. With a Labrador's ability to sniff, or register smells, for traces of explosives upward of 350 times per minute, they make ideal explosive detection dogs.

The Coast Guard cutter *Citrus*, a buoy tender converted into a medium-endurance cutter for law enforcement and search and rescue, sails into San Diego in 1985 after having been rammed by the Panamanian motor vessel *Pacific Star*. The *Citrus*, home-ported in Oregon, was operating approximately 700 miles southwest of San Diego when it attempted to board the *Pacific Star* and conduct a search for drugs. During the attempt to come alongside and prepare for boarding the crew, the *Pacific Star* drove their vessel into the *Citrus* and then proceeded to scuttle their vessel. The vessel was carrying marijuana and the crew hoped to sink the vessel with the drugs, but the *Citrus* was able to recover all seven crewmembers and approximately 1,000 pounds of marijuana. The *Citrus* was a 180-foot buoy tender commissioned in 1943 that remained in service until 1994.

The polar icebreaker *Polar Star* is photographed departing San Diego Bay after a port call in 1981. The *Polar Star*, one of three polar icebreaking cutters operated by the Coast Guard, was participating in Operation Deepfreeze, an operation that included icebreaking operations, bird/mammal surveys, seafloor soundings, sea temperature and salinity studies, and protein synthesis studies. The *Polar Star* and *Polar Sea* were commissioned in the late 1970s, while the Coast Guard cutter *Healy* was commissioned in 1999. While the polar icebreakers, or polar rollers as they are affectionately called, are capable of performing the Coast Guard missions of search and rescue, law enforcement, homeland security, etc., their primary roles are scientific research. They have berthing for teams of scientists, have research laboratories on board, and carry dive teams to collect and analyze data. In 1981, the *Polar Star* was conducting research in Winter Quarters Bay in Antarctica and made a port call in San Diego.

Three

COAST GUARD IN ACTION
RESCUES, BUSTS, AND TRAINING

"There I was on a dark and stormy night" or so the story usually starts when discussing some of the heroic rescues that Coasties have made. While San Diego weather usually does not provide the drama of "the perfect storm" type rescue, there have been many rescues over the years, each thrilling and dramatic in their own right. What San Diego does provide is ample opportunities for anti-smuggling operations. With the close proximity to Mexico, the San Diego Coast Guard has been on the front lines against smugglers since the inception of the air detachment in 1934. The primary mission of the air detachment was to patrol the borders, both land and sea, looking for smugglers. The aircraft initially flown by the detachment were in fact confiscated from the drug smugglers by customs.

This phone drop demonstration, photographed at the Air Station San Diego in 1948, shows a HO3S-1 Dragonfly hoisting down a telephone to a "survivor" on the ground. Lowering some form of communications to survivors is something still done today, except instead of a telephone line, it is a waterproof handheld radio.

Aircrew removes a patient on a litter from a PBY-5 in 1945. The PBY-5 was a converted navy aircraft, and the window the patient is being removed from actually served as a waist gunner position, with one located on each side. The Coast Guard used the windows, or "blisters," for increased field of view during search and rescue and removing patients.

Maintenance crews work to attach an external fuel tank to the left wing of a PBY-5A seaplane. The fuel tanks are used to extend the range of the search and rescue asset, whether it's a helicopter or airplane. The range of the PBY-5A could be extended to 4,000 miles with the use of the external tanks.

A young child is removed from a HSO4-1 helicopter on a litter while her mother looks on. Note how high above the cabin the pilots sat in the HSO4-1. The HSO4-1 was instrumental in the development of the use of helicopters for search and rescue, proving over and over again in the 1950s that the helicopter could be a valuable asset for years to come.

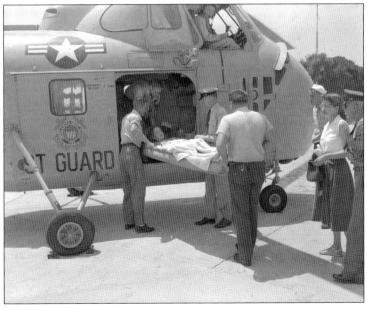

A HO4S-1 helicopter performs a search-and-rescue demonstration for crew and family members of the Coast Guard cutter *Androscoggin* during a dependants' cruise. The dependants' cruise, usually done on a yearly basis by Coast Guard cutters, gives the friends and family members of the crew a chance to experience life aboard a cutter for the day.

A Coast Guard HO4S-1 helicopter conducts a litter hoist from the vessel *Heroic* off the coast of San Diego in the early 1950s. The HO4S-1 was the first helicopter permanently stationed in San Diego after being purchased in 1951. Note the other boaters who have gathered for a front-row view of the medical evacuation.

Tie-down crews work to secure a HO4S-3G to the flight deck of a vessel outbound for sea in San Diego Bay. The tie-down crews work underneath a turning rotor without hearing or eye protection, something that is no longer accepted. Air Station San Diego hangars one and two are visible on the left side of the photograph.

A port security team of a Coastie and German shepherd conduct a beach patrol in 1944. The Coast Guard, responsible for maintaining port security, recruited members age 20–65 who were unable to serve on active duty to supplement the patrols. In this photograph the Coastie poses for a picture as he sites in on his Thompson machine gun.

A HH-3F responds to a search-and-rescue case and lands on the water. The flight mechanic can be seen kneeling on the platform trying to pull the survivor into the aircraft. The metal grate platform extends out into the water, making deployment and recovery of personnel from the water very easy.

A San Diego aircrew delivers a patient from a HH-52H to awaiting medical personnel on the San Diego ramp. Coast Guard rescue swimmers are level-two EMT certified and provide basic medical care to patients when picked up, but for more advanced medical care, the Coast Guard always transfers the patient to hospital or EMT staff.

Aviation Metalsmith (AM) Bob Ramsey (left) and Aviation Machinist Mate (AD) Joel Swart assemble the fittings for the Sikorsky HH-3F helicopter. The transmission, weighing in at 2,300 pounds, takes the power generated by the engines and reduces it to usable force to drive the main rotor head and the tail rotor. (Courtesy of Amy Goodpaster Strebe.)

A HH-65 is conducting helicopter in-flight refueling (HIFR) with a Coast Guard cutter off the coast of San Diego, preparing for a long-range search-and-rescue case. Flight crews utilize the rescue hoist to connect the fueling nozzle to the aircraft. Because the aircraft does not need to be shut down prior to fueling, this maneuver saves valuable time on a mission and extends the range of the helicopter.

The aircrew of CG-6561 poses in June 1995 after receiving an Air Medal for their actions on November 1, 1994. This San Diego aircrew performed the Coast Guard's first nighttime direct deployments to a vertical surface that evening in extreme fog conditions to successfully rescue two Mexican nationals trapped at the base of a rocky cliff south of Tijuana, Mexico, just as the high surf and waves threatened to knock them off the rocks. The aircrew received an Air Medal for the rescue and is pictured here at Miramar Naval Air Station after receiving the Order of Daedalians Outstanding Aircrew Rescue Award in June 1995. The Order of Daedalians is comprised of former military pilots, and each year they honor a Coast Guard crew from Air Station San Diego. From left to right are Lt. (jg) John Brenner, Aviation Machinist Mate Lane Clow, Aviation Survivalman Mario Marini, and Lt. Comdr. John Hardin. (Courtesy Mario Marini.)

A San Diego–based HH-60 Jayhawk prepares to lift a customs truck that fell into a ravine. The Jayhawk, a powerful helicopter with a cargo hook capability of 6,000 pounds, proved its versatility on this day, as it was able to lift the truck and deliver it without issue. This photograph was taken April 24, 2002.

On April 12, 2005, a Sector San Diego aviation survival technician practices vertical surface training off the coast of Point Loma, California. He is being lowered by a rescue hoist from a MH-60J Jayhawk. Although the Coast Guard primarily responds to search and rescue at sea, they are called upon to conduct inland search and rescue or cliff rescues off the coast.

Coast Guard crews pose with two Mexican fishermen who were rescued on December 26, 2006, after they spent five days at sea when their skiff overturned. The two men were rescued after they lit a smoke flare, drawing the attention of the aircrew. From left to right are Comdr. Sean Mahoney, Chief Ronny German, Lt. Vincent Jansen, Flight Mechanic Randy Marsh, Daniel Martinez-Gonzalez, Fernando Campos-Cruz, Lt. Iain McConnell, and Lt. Comdr. Chuck Bell.

CG-6037, a HH-60J Jayhawk, sits on the ramp at Lindbergh field during the San Diego fires of 2007. The CG-6037 was used to fly Department of Homeland Security secretary Michael Chertoff and California governor Arnold Schwarzenegger to survey the areas affected by the fires. A customs and border protection HH-60 sits in the background.

Crews from Small Boat Station San Diego conduct a medical evacuation of a man aboard the *Adventure Hornblower* in 2006. The Coast Guard performs an average of 90 medical evacuations a year in San Diego alone. On an ordinary day, all Coast Guard units around the world perform an average of 90 cases per day in addition to their other missions.

A crewmember of the Coast Guard cutter *Aspen* stands on a pier in San Diego after the crew offloaded over 8 tons of marijuana on March 22, 2008. The *Aspen*'s crewmembers, a C-130 crew from Air Station Sacramento and Maritime Safety and Security Team Galveston, worked with the Mexican Navy to seize over eight tons of marijuana and four smuggling suspects.

PO1 James B. Beard, an instructor from the Pacific Tactical Law Enforcement Team (PACTACLET), practices with the Japanese Maritime Self Defense Force (JMSDF) at a training facility in San Diego on June 6, 2008. The members from JMSDF are learning the basics of the Coast Guard's use of force, boarding procedures, weapons retention, and tactical procedures, along with physical fitness training.

PO1 Erin Stapleton serves as navigation plotter during special sea detail. Stapleton is responsible for determining the ship's position and ensuring safe navigation as the 378-foot cutter transits through San Diego Harbor. The picture is taken aboard the Coast Guard cutter *Hamilton* stationed in San Diego, California, at Naval Base San Diego.

Comdr. Sean Cross, Lt. Simon Greene, Aviation Maintenance Technician 2c Jonathan Randolph, and Aviation Survival Technician 3c Robyn Hamilton, shown from left to right, receive an Air Medal for a long-range rescue completed December 13–14, 2008. The crew flew approximately 600 nautical miles west of San Diego, through a Pacific winter storm, to rescue a crewman suffering from a life-threatening head trauma. The crew flew the first 285 nautical miles to the USS *Abraham Lincoln* where they refueled the helicopter and embarked two U.S. Navy medical personnel. They then flew another 250 nautical miles to the vessel with the injured crewman. Battling 30-knot winds and 15- to 20-foot seas, they successfully hoisted the injured crewmember, avoiding numerous obstacles on the ship's pitching deck. The crew flew another 250 nautical miles back to the USS *Abraham Lincoln*. When the crew had finally landed, they had been awake for over 24 hours, flown 750 nautical miles, logged 7 hours of flight time, and most importantly, saved the life of the injured crewman.

Flight deck personnel ready a San Diego Coast Guard MH-60J for launch at dawn on the flight deck aboard USS *Abraham Lincoln* (CVN 72). The helicopter participated in a rescue in which an injured merchant sailor was medically evacuated to Lincoln and stabilized before being flown to San Francisco for treatment. (U.S. Navy photograph by Mass Communication Specialist 2nd Class James R. Evans/Released.)

PO3 Christopher Brewer serves as bearing taker during special sea detail on the Coast Guard cutter *Hamilton* as it transits through San Diego Bay. The bearings he takes are passed via sound-powered phone to the navigation plotter, who will use them to determine the cutter's position.

Coast Guard petty officers practice tossing a life ring just off of Ballast Point. The art of seamanship is stressed to all who are stationed aboard boats and ships and even with their busy patrols schedules, Coasties always find time to refine and practice the skills required. A life ring such as this would be tossed during man overboard drills or to survivors found during a search-and-rescue case.

Coast Guard cutter *Haddock* towed the sailing vessel *Sea Hag* into San Diego Harbor April 6, 2009, after an extensive search. The owner of the vessel had been sailing for a number of weeks, and when he did not arrive in San Diego as expected, his family members contacted the Coast Guard. Once found, the *Haddock* was diverted to the location and brought the vessel and captain safely into port.

PO1 Nicholas Muscolo, an electronics technician stationed at Electronics Support Detachment (ESD) San Diego, climbs a communication tower on July 30, 2009. ESD San Diego Conducts tower climbing and rescue training with Coast Guard Reserve members from Alameda and San Pedro. Electronics technicians must maintain a climbing proficiency to reach the communication equipment they service and repair at the tops of towers and ships' masts.

PO3 Joseph Nelson (right), an aviation maintenance technician, teaches airman Ryan Tennis how to inspect the hoist cable of an MH-60J Jayhawk helicopter at Coast Guard Sector San Diego on July 22, 2009. The cable must be checked frequently to ensure it is free of fraying, kinks, or damage of any kind and is safe to use.

A Coast Guard MH-60 Jayhawk conducts a medical evacuation of an ill man on the Norwegian cruise ship *Norwegian Wind* in 2006. The port of San Diego is a port of call for over 300 cruise ships per year. Those in need of a medical evacuation while sailing around Baja, Mexico, to Los Angeles, California, will be flown to a hospital by crews from Coast Guard Sector San Diego.

The Coast Guard conducted a medical evacuation from a commercial fishing boat 80 miles south of Point Loma, California, on July 3, 2009. The Joint Harbor Operations Center dispatched an MH-60 helicopter from Sector San Diego to conduct the hoist and transport the patient back to the base where emergency medical services were standing by.

CWO Joel Mason (left), from Coast Guard Sector San Diego, and Ens. Kenn Yuen (right), from the Coast Guard Cutter *Chase*, compare notes after conducting an inspection on the sailing ship *Star of India* while it was in dry dock on September 2, 2009. The *Star of India* is the world's oldest active sailing ship built in 1863 in the Isle of Man, Great Britain.

The Coast Guard medically evacuated a 26-year-old man from the cruise ship *Carnival Elation* 4 miles off the coast of San Diego on September 8, 2009. PO3 Paul Ramos, a boatswain's mate from Station San Diego, examines a man in the cabin of a 41-foot utility boat. The cruise ship met the Coast Guard at the San Diego Bay entrance buoy and transferred the man.

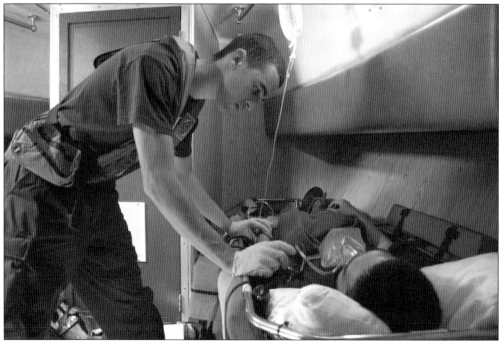

The Coast Guard cutter *Petrel* returns to Sector San Diego with 23 illegal migrants apprehended on September 16, 2009. The migrants were found near Ponto Beach, California, with the help of customs and border protection and the San Diego County Sheriff's Department. On an average day, the Coast Guard interdicts 17 illegal migrants at sea.

Coast Guard Sector San Diego's Incident Management Division conducts a drill with the San Diego Lifeguards in conjunction with the San Diego Regional Aquatic Lifesaving Emergency Response Taskforce (SDR ALERT) in 2009. This is a multiagency mass-casualty drill conducted on Moonlight Beach in Encinitas, California. This taskforce is designed to help San Diego area emergency response agencies work together more efficiently.

Sector San Diego pilots and aircrew meet their annual flight-training requirements known as "wet drills." Members wear their dry suit (worn by aircrew when the water temperature is less than 70°F) and survival vest. They test the rubber seals of the dry suit to make sure that they fit properly and there are no leaks, swim 75 yards in the open ocean, and climb into a life raft.

PO1 Keith Knoop, stationed aboard the Coast Guard cutter *Edisto* whose homeport is San Diego, was awarded the Coast Guard Commendation Medal on October 2, 2009, for administering CPR and saving the life of three-year-old Makenna McKamey, who he holds in his arms following the award ceremony.

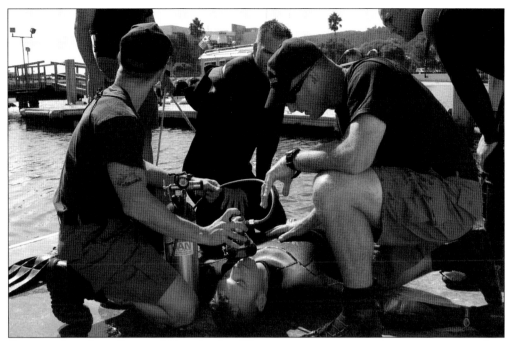

Crewmembers from Regional Dive Locker West participate in a mock emergency procedure drill at Naval Submarine Base Point Loma on October 20, 2009. Crewmembers conduct drills to maintain their training, knowledge, and proficiency in the event of an actual emergency. Here they are simulating a diver injury and are ready to give him oxygen.

PO1 Krista M. Stacey, a boarding officer from Station San Diego, asks a boater some questions before conducting a boarding of their vessel to ensure the owner/operator is in compliance with all federal laws and regulations. Stacey is a reservist currently serving on active duty.

A helicopter crew conducts rescue hoist training with a 41-foot utility boat. Air and boat crews conduct training on a weekly basis, challenging themselves with real life scenarios in order to be ready when the real situation arises. The pride crews take in their work is reflected on the back of the flight mechanic's helmet. It says "The Hallmark crew: When you care to send the very best."

A rescue swimmer sits in the door preparing for a free-fall deployment to the water in San Diego's South Bay. A free-fall deployment is made from below 15 feet and in daytime conditions only, as the rescue swimmer literally allows himself to fall in the seated position into the water. It is a dangerous maneuver and requires a lot of coordination between the pilots and crew.

A San Diego HH-60 Jayhawk sits on the ramp at the Coast Guard Aviation Training Center in Mobile, Alabama, in September 2005. Air Station San Diego sent two helicopters and several aircrew members to Mobile in support of Hurricane Katrina, as Coasties from all over the country converged to work around the clock in the rescue and recovery efforts. In all, Air Station San Diego aircrews and helicopters were in Mobile for seven days in support of Hurricane Katrina. In the below photograph, Lt. Dave Marrama pilots the Jayhawk from the right seat with hurricane-ravaged New Orleans visible in the background.

Small Boat Station San Diego's three 33-foot special purpose craft cruise in formation past *Zuniga Jetty*. The 33-foot boats, powered by three outboard engines, are capable of almost 60 miles per hour and can carry up to 10 crewmembers and passengers. It is the perfect vessel for chasing drug smugglers.

Ens. Elisabeth Bosma reaches for her weapon during pepper spray training. The training, which all Coast Guard boarding team members must undergo at least once in their careers, involves being sprayed in the eyes with pepper spray and then having to react when attacked and take down the assailant. Most Coasties make several copies of the letter certifying completion of this training to ensure they never have to experience it again.

Small boat station crewmembers pose with marijuana they recovered in a drug bust on April 21, 2008. The Coast Guard has unique law enforcement authorities on the waterways that allow for searches, seizures, and arrests without necessitating a warrant. Stopping drug smugglers is one of the prominent missions found in the San Diego area.

A C-130 from Air Station Sacramento waits on deck at Lindbergh Field during the San Diego fires of October 2007. The C-130 was delivering food, water, and cots to San Diego for the many shelters located throughout San Diego County. The Coast Guard's role during the fires included transporting senior leadership and relief supplies.

The Sector San Diego Honor Guard renders a 21-gun salute during the funeral of Captain F. Montali, the air station's commanding officer from 1979 to 1982. This photograph was taken at Fort Rosecrans National Cemetery. Naval Air Station North Island and the Coronado Bridge can be seen in the background. The Honor Guard renders honors at approximately two funerals per month.

A Coast Guard MH-60 helicopter takes off from Air Station San Diego as smoke from wildfires obscures the sunrise. Coast Guard personnel and aircraft participated in wildfire response operations throughout Southern California in 2007. The fire crews, from Training Center Petaluma, were in the San Diego area to assist in fighting the wildfires as well.

Four

A STRONG FOUNDATION
THE DEVELOPMENT OF THE BASE

From the humble beginnings of the air detachment based out of Lindbergh Field, today's Coast Guard Sector San Diego has come a long way. The base now includes an air station, a prevention department responsible for marine inspections and waterway management, a small boat station, many administrative and support functions for surrounding units, and is the homeport for four patrol boats. The development of the base has been gradual over the years, often out of necessity as the missions have grown and evolved. The history of San Diego and the Coast Guard are intertwined; as the city of San Diego has developed, so too has the Coast Guard.

This photograph is from pre–air station days when the air detachment was based out of Lindbergh Field. The AirTech commercial building was used as a base of operations and can be seen in the background. On the ramp, the RD-4 fixed-wing aircraft, flown by the air detachment beginning in 1934, sits ready for a mission.

U.S. COAST GUARD AIR STATION   SAN DIEGO, CAL.   4-7-37

This is one of the oldest buildings on the Coast Guard base, taken on April 7, 1937. Today this building is used for the duty crew rooms, the officer wardroom, a conference room, the educations services office, and locker rooms. Duty aircrew (pilot, copilot, rescue swimmer, and flight mechanic), the sector duty officer, and the aviation watch captain all remain on base for a 24-hour watch.

This aerial shot of Lindbergh Field and Pacific Highway in 1937 is at the time of the air station's commissioning. The white building with "AIR TECH" written across the front is the building that was used for the air detachment from 1934 to 1937 prior to the air station moving to its permanent location. Note that the Embarcadero waterfront has not been built up yet.

Construction of the air station began in 1936 with funds provided by the Federal Public Works Administration. The area was filled and brought up to grade level by dredging from the bay. Long piles were driven into the soil at the building sites for stabilization. During construction, the Air Patrol Detachment continued to operate out of Lindbergh Field. In April 1937, Coast Guard Air Station San Diego was commissioned.

This photograph shows the administration building, constructed in 1935, one of the original buildings on the base. It has been renovated and expanded several times and now is home to the command front office, the master chief, the chaplain, and the servicing personnel office. The servicing personnel office handles the administrative responsibilities for all San Diego area Coasties, including those stationed on ships.

The original hangar, or hangar 1 as it's called, that was constructed in 1935 when the base was commissioned is used today as the maintenance hangar, housing helicopters during heavy maintenance periods. It also contains the base gym and administrative offices for the patrol boats. The second hangar, or hangar 2, can be seen off to the right and was constructed in 1944.

A port security recruiting office is shown in San Diego during World War II. The Coast Guard found port security to be a heavy drain on manpower during the war years. In order to supplement the active duty force, a volunteer port security force was established that allowed men and women who were not eligible for military service and between the ages of 20–65 to serve.

This is the main gate of Coast Guard Air Station San Diego during World War II. In the background is a PBY-5A. Until September 11, 2001, most of the base did not have security fences. With the new mission of homeland security, the Coast Guard increased its security measures in and around the base.

This photograph was taken in 1949. Notice the helicopter ramp is in the process of being constructed for the arrival of helicopters in 1951. The galley and the bachelor officer quarters (constructed 1954) and the racquetball court (constructed 1950) are not present. Lindbergh Field can be seen across the street. Note the lack of traffic on Harbor Drive.

Pictured is Ballast Point Light Station in the 1950s. The lighthouse was built at the tip of Point Loma in 1891 and has been owned and operated by the Coast Guard ever since. It serves today as an active navigational aide and government housing for high-ranking Coast Guard officers in the San Diego area.

This aerial view of the ramp was most likely taken in the 1950s, as both hangars are constructed, and there is a helicopter ramp with a HO4S-1 helicopter on deck in the upper half of the photograph with three PBM seaplanes and an PBY-5A still present. (Seaplanes went out of service in 1960.)

The air station's original bell was used to sound the alarm when a search-and-rescue launch was required. While the bell has long since been replaced by a more modern alarm that is sounded with the base's public address system, it remains on the base as a reminder of days gone by and is now located near the flagpole. The bell is engraved with the date of commissioning.

Pictured is hangar 2 at Coast Guard Air Station San Diego. In the hangar, flight mechanics are performing routine maintenance on the HUS-1G Seahorse. More than four HUS-1G Seahorses could fit in the hangar together; however, the hangar can only accommodate a maximum of three MH-60J Jayhawk helicopters. The sliding hangar doors pictured are still in use today.

Ballast Point is seen here in June 1968. Ballast Point, located on the anti-submarine warfare navy base, serves as the home to two San Diego–based patrol boats and has been built up to be able to support the boats and their crew. Point Loma is seen in the background.

An aerial view of Ballast Point is shown from January 2007. Over the years there have been several buildings added in support of the patrol boats that call Ballast Point their home. Note how the layout of the point looks completely different than it did in the 1968 aerial photograph.

Point Loma Lighthouse, with Coast Guard housing in the background, is seen in the 1970s. The property, situated on beautiful Point Loma, is the home for the senior-ranking Coast Guard officers in the San Diego area. Point Loma Lighthouse was originally located higher up on the point, but during poor visibility, the light became obscured. In 1891, the current lighthouse was constructed and placed into service.

A cake celebrating the commissioning of the marine safety office at the base is shown here in December 1974. The marine inspectors office had been located at the Broadway Street Pier and then on B Street until 1974. The commanding officer of the Marine Safety Office San Diego held two regulatory positions: officer in charge of marine inspections and captain of the port. This title and authority remained in place until 2004, when Activities San Diego reorganized to become Sector San Diego.

Most of the buildings that are present today have been constructed by the time this aerial photograph of the base was taken in 1981. Most glaringly absent is the Joint Harbor Operations Center/small boat station building that would later be constructed in 1982. Note the absence of a security fence around the perimeter of the base. The security fence was not put into place until after the September 11, 2001, attacks.

This is an aerial view of Coast Guard Group San Diego, as it was called in the 1980s. This picture was taken in the time frame of late 1984 to early 1985. Group San Diego consisted of Small Boat Station San Diego, Marine Safety Office San Diego, and Air Station San Diego. Group San Diego later became Activities San Diego.

Coast Guard Air Station San Diego is celebrating its 50th year in San Diego. The photograph was taken in 1987 with air station personnel, a HU-25 Falcon, and a HH-65 Dolphin. The base was established in 1934 as an air patrol detachment. In 1937, it became an official Coast Guard Air Station under the command of Lt. S. C. Linholm. At this time, it was the only Coast Guard base in California.

This building, constructed in 1982 as a multipurpose building, houses the Joint Harbor Operations Center, the operations, planning, and administrative departments. The Joint Harbor Operations Center (JHOC) serves as the command center for the base and is manned 24 hours a day, seven days a week by a watch that is comprised of several different agencies. Each case that is handled by the Coast Guard in San Diego is run from this facility.

The base galley, built in 1954, provides an affordable, on-base option for breakfast, lunch, and dinner each day of the week. Currently manned by a contractor, the galley serves close to 300 meals a day and caters several of the on-base picnics throughout the year. While the meal rates have gone up over the years, they remain very affordable with $2.30 for breakfast and $4.25 for lunch/dinner.

The administration building houses the Servicing Personnel Office, the post office, the command offices, and the chaplain's office. The Servicing Personnel Office (SPO), formerly known as the Personnel Reporting Unit (PERSRU), is responsible for all the administrative duties of the base. These include pay, leave, in- and out-processing, awards, and orders. The chaplain is a navy chaplain assigned to the Coast Guard and serves the entire Southern California region.

The Prevention building, formerly known as the Marine Safety Office (MSO), was built in 1974. The Prevention Department is responsible for all aspects of the Marine Safety Mission and Aids to Navigation in San Diego County and the Colorado River, including its surrounding lakes. More specifically, the Prevention Department oversees inspections of domestic and foreign commercial vessels, inspection of maritime facilities, investigations of maritime casualties and accidents, and safe navigation and usage of the waterways.

This building, erected in 1937, houses the senior officer quarters, the wardroom, and the duty rooms for the aircrew. The wardroom serves as both a meeting room and a place for social gatherings. The duty rooms provide a place for the aircrew on duty to sleep during the night, while still being ready to launch on a case within the required 30-minute window.

The original hangar built in 1935 is shown as it appears today. Now serving as the maintenance hangar for helicopters undergoing scheduled work, it has an electric hoist mounted in the ceiling that is used to lift the heavy parts of the helicopter, such as the transmission. The metal shop, where all welding is performed, is also located in this hangar.

This second hangar was constructed during World War II and completed in 1944. It serves as the main hangar for storing the "ready" helicopters in addition to housing the offices for aviation engineering, supply, public affairs, work life, and a training room for all-hands training. A designated paint locker also provides a space for all paintwork.

The guard shack is located at the base point of entry. Built in 2001 to replace the older shack when base security was beefed up following the September 11 attacks, the gate monitors all traffic on and off the base. The entry is manned by junior enlisted personnel who verify the identification of each person coming onto the base.

The main door to the small boat station is located on the first floor of the Joint Harbor Operations Center building. The small boat station was commissioned in 1994 and has a complement of approximately 40 members. The station uses 41-foot utility boats and 33-foot fast-response boats to accomplish search and rescue and law enforcement in the San Diego and Mission Bays.

California governor Arnold Schwarzenegger is pictured at the ribbon-cutting ceremony marking the official opening of the Joint Harbor Operations Center (JHOC) at Coast Guard Sector San Diego in 2005. The JHOC supports our maritime homeland security strategy by unifying our protection efforts, enabling effective partnerships, developing complementary and interconnected systems, and ensuring that essential requirements are met.

The armory houses the small arms for the base. It is run by a complement of Gunners Mates (GM) who coordinates training and qualifications in both rifles and pistols for the San Diego area Coast Guard units. Coast Guard members must be proficient in the use of small arms for the purpose of self-defense and must complete an in-depth training syllabus before being allowed to carry weapons.

Located where the old reserve building used to be, the pavilion serves as an ideal place to hold an outdoor or just a good old-fashioned picnic. It also serves as a place for law enforcement training where Coasties can train with each other and other agencies on tactics and procedures used during boardings.

The unit patch is a military staple, often a creation of the unit and designed to be worn on the uniform, whether a flight suit, ball cap, or coveralls. This montage displays the various unit patches that have existed in San Diego dating back to the 1960s. Covering the variety of units that have called San Diego home, the patches include the small boat station, the air station, the Marine

Safety Office, Group San Diego, Activities San Diego, and finally, Sector San Diego. The patches are quite popular and are often in high demand when the Coast Guard is represented at an air show or public demonstration. (Patches courtesy of Lt. Comdr. Rex M. Wessling, ret.)

This aerial photograph featuring the beautiful San Diego skyline shows Sector San Diego in present day. The major changes that have occurred to the base since this 1981 aerial photograph was taken are the presence of the Joint Harbor Operations Center/small boat station building and the absence of the reservist building. In 2007, most of the trees on the base had to be removed due to the root structure damaging the historic buildings.

Five

COASTIE PORTRAITS
A LOOK AT THOSE WHO SERVE

The men and women of the Coast Guard proudly serve their country on a daily basis, fulfilling a variety of different professional roles to accomplish the many missions demanded of them. The Coast Guard, the smallest of the five armed services, accomplishes its many missions with a force smaller than the New York City police department. The procedures and techniques that have been developed through the years have been written in blood and passed down to each Coastie. Each and every Coastie is an important part of the team and integral to accomplishing the mission safely and efficiently.

This photograph, dated in 1935, is the San Diego Air Detachment posing in front of the JF-2 Duck and the RD-2 Dolphin. Note the AirTech hangar, which is the commercial hangar at Lindbergh field the air detachment was based out of until moving to the base in 1937. The commanding officer in this picture is believed to be Lieutenant Christopher, the first commanding officer of the air detachment from 1934 to 1935.

Lt. Stanley C. Linholm was the first commanding officer of Air Station San Diego. Lieutenant Linholm, the 36th Coastie to be winged a naval aviator, replaced Comdr. E. F. Stone upon his death while serving as the commanding officer of the air detachment. Lieutenant Linholm would become the commanding officer of the Biloxi Coast Guard Air Station and later served as the commander of the Eleventh Coast Guard District.

Comdr. Frank A. Leamy was the air station commanding officer from 1939 to 1940. Commander Leamy would go on to serve as the aviation operations officer at Coast Guard Headquarters and later as the superintendent of the Coast Guard Academy. He retired in 1960 as a rear admiral and is buried in Arlington National Cemetery.

Comdr. Watson A. Burton was commanding officer of Air Station San Diego from 1942 to 1944. Commander Burton was an influential figure in the development of the helicopter for Coast Guard use. He was present on April 20, 1942, in Stratford, Connecticut, to observe a helicopter test. Commander Burton was so impressed with the capabilities of the helicopter that in his report he recommended the Coast Guard purchase three for training and development.

Captain Linholm, who served as the first commanding officer of Air Station San Diego from 1936 to 1939, presides over a personnel inspection at Air Station Elizabeth City in 1949 or 1950. Personnel inspections, an ancient military tradition, allow the commanding officer a firsthand look at the fitness and appearance of his unit. Executive Officer Richard Mellen is seen behind Captain Linholm.

Coasties celebrate Coast Guard Day on August 4, 1944. The Coast Guard was established on August 4, 1790, as the Revenue Cutter Service and the birthday of the service is celebrated each year at all Coast Guard units, often accompanied by a picnic and helicopter demonstrations. Note that in 1944, the men and women ate separately in the galley.

Comdr. (later Capt.) Donald B. MacDiarmid served as the air station commanding officer from 1944 to 1947 and then again from 1949 to 1952. MacDiarmid arrived shortly after the new national search-and-rescue plan was implemented. He was a major proponent of seaplanes and spent many years trying to prove they could be landed successfully at sea. Eventually the helicopter won out, and the Coast Guard stopped using seaplanes in 1960.

As a retirement gift for the retiring maintenance officer, the mechanics take a moment to pose for a humorous photograph. The sign being held up advertises for "Wally's wrecking works," with new and used helicopters for sale and unbeatable financing options. The helicopters sitting in hangar 1 are HSO4s, indicating this photograph to be dated in the 1950s.

Hollywood starlet Lola Albright poses for a picture with Air Station Commanding Officer Capt. Bob Waldron on a 1961 visit to the air station. Albright, a multitalented actress and singer, was nominated for an Emmy for Best Supporting Actress in 1959 for her role as Edie Hart in the television detective series *Peter Gunn*. She also released two albums, one in 1957 and the other in 1959.

A nightshift female mechanic (name unknown) sits atop a Sikorsky HH-52A in the 1970s. The Coast Guard has allowed women in the service since 1918 and has never discriminated between what jobs are available to men or women. Today women serve as mechanics, electricians, pilots, divers, and executive/commanding officers.

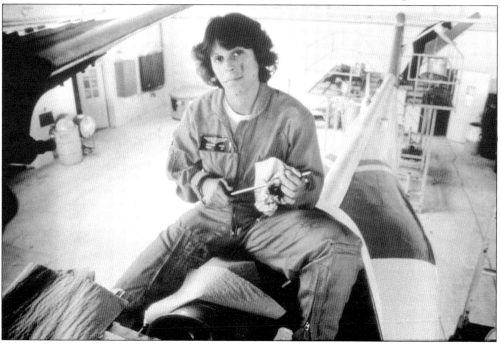

The members of Air Station San Diego's Aviation Survivalman (ASM) Shop, or rescue swimmers, pose in front of a HH-65 Dolphin in 1993. The Coast Guard's rescue swimmer program began in the mid-1980s and involves intense physical and mental training. From left to right are (first row) Gary Strebe and Jose Baldwin; (second row) ASMs Mario Marini, Jeff Marsh, Marc Galbraith, Jason Orsborne, Reed Breitenstein, and Brad Torrens. (Courtesy Mario Marini.)

From left to right, Aviation Survivalmen (ASM) Marc Galbraith, Dale Knutsen, and Mario Marini pose in their gear after being awarded the first ASM Shop San Diego "DFC" (Distinguished Floor Cleaning award) in 1992. The term DFC usually refers to the Distinguished Flying Cross, an award most aircrew dream of receiving for taking part in a daring and dangerous rescue. (Courtesy Mario Marini.)

A Coast Guard aircrew takes a moment to pose with Smokey the Bear at the American Heroes air show just outside of Los Angeles, California. Coast Guard aircraft are always a popular attraction and Air Station San Diego strives to participate in as many air shows as possible, appearing in approximately 10 each year. From left to right are Lt. Rick Hipes, Lieutenant Menze, PO Adam Sustachek, and PO Henri Bradley.

Camera crews from the motion picture the *Guardian*, starring Ashton Kutcher and Kevin Costner, filmed at Coast Guard Sector San Diego in 2005. On the set is Comdr. Kevin Raimer from the Coast Guard Motion Picture Office in Los Angeles, California. The movie depicted the challenges of a Coast Guard Rescue Swimmer. The movie was released on September 26, 2006.

Children from Francis Parker Elementary School come to Coast Guard Sector San Diego for a tour of the facilities, boats, and helicopters. Eight children are sitting in a rescue basket found in a MH-60 Jayhawk helicopter. The rescue basket can lift up to 600 pounds and is the primary rescue device used. Unless under an extreme emergency, only one person is hoisted in the rescue basket at a time.

Sector San Diego Coasties form up during a memorial ceremony for Coast Guard helicopter CG-6505. The CG-6505, an HH-65 Dolphin, was lost during a training accident in on the night of September 4, 2008, off the coast of Honolulu, Hawaii. Capt. Thomas Nelson, Lt. Comdr. Andrew Wischmeier, AST David Skimin, and AMT Joshua Nichols all lost their lives during the accident. This ceremony was held on April 8, 2009.

Prior to a memorial service honoring the crew of CG-6505 that crashed off Barbers Point, Hawaii, in 2008, five Coast Guard ensigns were mailed to each air station. As they traveled the United States, each air station would take at least two photographs with the ensigns and then pass the flags on to the next air station. The last stop was Barbers Point, Hawaii, for the memorial service.

The Tuskegee Airmen visited the air station on February 14, 2007 and delivered a presentation on the history of the Tuskegee Airmen in World War II. The San Diego chapter is named after Gen. B. O. Davis, who became the first African American general in the U.S. Air Force. From left to right are George T. Mitchell, Thurman Pirtle, Bob Maxwell, and Dave Marrama.

Members of aviation maintenance are shown working on the mighty HH-60J. For every one hour of flight time, 28 hours of maintenance is performed to keep the helicopters up and running. From left to right are AMTs Brian Sickler, Ramon Marion, Joe Nelson, Guillermo Melendez-Gaitan, John Randolph, and Ryan Banks.

Members of the Chilean Navy pose for a photograph in front of an HH-60J in hangar 2. This particular visit occurred in June 2006 and was part of a yearly program for Chilean Navy personnel to become familiar with the U.S. Coast Guard. Visits from foreign militaries are common and present the opportunity for international camaraderie.

Rudolph and Santa arrive for the annual children's Christmas party, held every December in the hangar. Since the 1980s, Santa, Rudolph, and the elves have been arriving bearing gifts delivered by helicopter to the delight of the children. The downtown San Diego skyline is on display in the background in this photograph taken in December 2006.

Coast Guard members from the Aids to Navigation Team San Diego and the USCGC *Zephyr* train U.S. Naval Sea Cadets in 2007. The Naval Sea Cadet Corps (NSCC) is for American youths age 13–17 who have a desire to learn about the U.S. Navy, Marine Corps, Coast Guard, and Merchant Marine. The sea cadet program is designed to introduce youth to naval life.

Members from Coast Guard Sector San Diego attend the Miramar Air Show in October 2008: (from left to right) LTJG Philip Granati, Lt. Jeremy Denning, PA3 Jetta Disco, and AMT2 Steven Conrad. As *your* Coast Guard, we want to forge the strongest possible relationships with those we serve. Air shows can be exciting and educational events that bring together the entire community.

Camera crews from the Discovery Channel show *Deadliest Catch* film "After the Catch" featuring Capt. Sig Hansen from the fishing vessel *Northwestern*. Capt. Sig Hansen experienced firsthand what a helicopter rescue by the Coast Guard is all about, as he watched a search-and-rescue demonstration from the back of a MH-60 from Sector San Diego. The crew is pictured briefing before their flight.

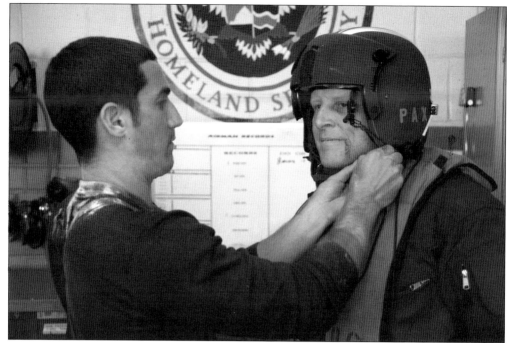

Rescue swimmer Scott Mochkatel fits television's *Deadliest Catch* Capt. Sig Hanson for a flight helmet in the survival shop. Captain Hanson, a fishing boat captain, was filming a season wrap-up show in San Diego and was able to get up in the back of a HH-60J Jayhawk to observe rescue training operations from the Coast Guard perspective.

On March 11, 2008, members of the Coast Guard Academy Glee Club perform in the center of Seaport Village in downtown San Diego Harbor. The cadets perform at several locations throughout the city on their spring-break tour. Members of the glee club range from third class cadets (sophomores) to first class cadets (seniors) at the academy.

PO2 Michael Dalager, a reservist at the Aids to Navigation Team, San Diego, sings "God Bless America" at the San Diego Padres baseball game on July 4. The stadium was sold out, as more than 42,000 fans attended the Fourth of July event. The Padres are strong supporters of the military in San Diego.

Lt. Vincent Jansen, of Sector San Diego, focuses on his target before firing a 45-caliber pistol during the 2008 U.S. Navy Pacific Fleet Forces Pistol Match held at Marine Corps Base Camp Pendleton. During individual and team events, eight members from Coast Guard Pacific area commands competed against participants from the navy, Marine Corps, and retired military.

Families and members of the Coast Guard Port Security Unit (PSU) enjoy a picnic lunch during a family day at Coast Guard Sector San Diego prior to the unit's deployment on November 30, 2008. PSU 311 is a highly deployable, expeditionary/coastal warfare unit that provides a specialized capability focused on securing foreign ports during military contingencies and protecting high-value assets from waterborne incursions.

Lt. Simon Greene, an MH-60 Jayhawk pilot stationed at Sector San Diego, hits a softball during a game against the Navy Joint Tactical Radio System Unit at the anti-submarine warfare softball field on June 8, 2009. Sector San Diego's softball team plays against various teams twice a week during their season.

Capt. Charles "Chip" Strangfeld, commanding officer of Coast Guard Sector San Diego from 2005 to 2008, sits atop a border patrol horse during a tour of the border facilities. The Coast Guard works closely with their fellow Department of Homeland Security agencies, including border patrol, to keep the border and this country safe.

Lt. Sonja Hedrick and Ens. Eric Woynaroski weigh bags of trash and recyclables on April 25, 2009, during the Seventh Annual Creek to Bay cleanup day in Chula Vista, California. Coast Guard members and their families, Sea Partners, and other local volunteers donated several hours of their time to help keep the San Diego coastline clean. More than 4,000 volunteers participated throughout San Diego County.

Lt. Reyna Hernandez, the commanding officer of the Coast Guard cutter *Haddock*, and the crew of the *Haddock* show off their prize, the trophy for first place in the 87-foot patrol boat roundup. Events included seamanship, dewatering, sports, and a chili cook-off. The roundup is a morale booster for the 87-foot patrol boats in the San Diego area.

Rescue swimmers Logan Banner and Robyn Hamilton get a cardio workout on the stationary bike. In the background, airmen Justin James and Jonathan Kreske look on. Being a rescue swimmer is physically demanding, and they are required to stay in top physical shape with mandatory workouts each day. Airmen are prospective rescue swimmers who must spend 90 days at an air station before they can commence rescue swimmer training.

From left to right, Lt. Ari Fitzwater, Lt. William Mees, and Capt. Thomas Farris salute during the Coast Guard cutter *Edisto*'s change-of-command ceremony on July 17, 2009. Command of the *Edisto*, a 110-foot patrol boat whose missions include maritime law enforcement, search and rescue, migrant interdiction, and coastal defense, was transferred from Mees to Fitzwater.

Coasties Robyn Hamilton, Kristen Beer, Brian Lee, and Annina Iobst line up with other military honorees at the San Diego Padres' military appreciation pre-game ceremony. Each year the Padres honor select members of each service who have been recognized for their performance during the preceding year. Each of these Coasties had been recognized by their command for demonstrating outstanding leadership and devotion to duty.

Honorary "Chief" Jake Bath shakes hands with the crew of the Coast Guard cutter *Petrel*. Jake was provided the opportunity to experience the Coast Guard for a day in October 2008 through the Make a Wish foundation. In addition to being granted the title of honorary chief, Jake was able to get underway with the crew of the *Petrel* and tour a HH-60J Jayhawk.

Members from Sector San Diego Public Affairs and District 11 Public Affairs Detachment receive first place in the prestigious Comdr. Jim Simpson Award for excellence in Coast Guard Public Affairs for 2008. From left to right are Lt. Joshua Nelson, Lt. Jeremy Denning, Lt. (jg) Amanda Sardone, PO1 Allyson Conroy, PO2 Jetta Disco, and PO3 Henry Dunphy.

Six

COMDR. ELMER F. STONE
AVIATOR AND OFFICER

Comdr. Elmer F. Stone is one of the most colorful figures in Coast Guard aviation history. Having graduated as an officer of the Revenue Cutter Service in 1913, he served aboard multiple ships as an engineer and line officer. In 1916, he requested an aviation assignment and was sent to aviation training with the navy in Pensacola, Florida. He was "winged" as the Coast Guard's first naval aviator in April 1917.

His first remarkable achievement occurred in 1919 when, as the pilot in command of navy seaplane NC-4, he and his crew completed the first-ever transatlantic flight for which he was awarded the Navy Cross. During the 1920s, he continued to work with the U.S. Navy to develop carrier flight deck operation techniques and would later serve as the commanding officer of the Coast Guard destroyers *Monaghan* and *Cummings*.

In the early 1930s, he served as a senior board member for the development of Coast Guard seaplanes and later set the world record (at that time) for an amphibian airplane at 191 miles per hour. In the spring of 1935, he reported for duty as the second commanding officer of Coast Guard Air Detachment San Diego; a job he would hold until his death of a heart attack in 1936.

Comdr. E. F. Stone truly set an example for not just aviators, but all Coasties who have followed him.

Comdr. Elmer F. Stone (1887–1936) was the first Coast Guard aviator to receive his "Wings of Gold" from naval flight training in 1917, designating him a naval aviator. In 1919, he was a pilot aboard the navy seaplane that completed the first transatlantic flight, completing a journey from Rockaway, New York, to Plymouth, England. Commander Stone was the first commanding officer of Air Patrol Detachment San Diego from 1935 to 1936. Stone had a long history for service to the Coast Guard beginning in 1913, when he graduated from the Revenue Cutter Service Academy. His first assignment was on board the Revenue cutter *Onondaga*, and he was detailed to study the steam machinery of the vessel. On October 9, 1914, Stone was transferred to *Itasca*, on which vessel he served until February 1, 1915, when he was again assigned to *Onondaga*. It was while he was serving aboard *Onondaga* that he participated in the rescue of seven seamen who had been shipwrecked on the lumber-laden schooner C. C. *Wehrum* off False Cape, Virginia. From there, Stone started his aviation career.

fédération aéronautique internationale

siège social : 6, rue galilée, paris

diplôme de record

nous soussignés certifions que le Lt Commandr. *Elmer F. Stone*
sur amphibie Grumman JF-2 N° 167
de U. S. Coast Guard, moteur Wright "Cyclone" **a établi le** 20 Décembre 1934 **le**

record suivant : *Vitesse sur base (308 kms 567)*

_____ Classe C. ter _____

à Hampton Roads, Virginia.

le président de la f. a. i. :

pour le National Aeronautic Association
of U.S.A.
le président :

le secrétaire général :

Paul Tissandier

Comdr. Elmer F. Stone climbs out of a Coast Guard Grumman JF-2 V167. During his illustrious career, Commander Stone was instrumental in the development and testing of several important contributions to naval and Coast Guard aviation. In the early 1920s, he served as a test pilot for the navy and provided valuable input on the development of catapult and deck-arresting equipment for aircraft carriers. In this photograph, he is seen on December 20, 1934, after establishing a new world speed record for seaplanes in which he travelled over a 1.8-mile test course and reached a speed of 191 miles per hour. The certificate signifying his accomplishment is shown below.

Commander Stone sits at his desk at Air Station Cape May, New Jersey. Commander Stone served as the commanding officer of Air Station Cape May from the spring of 1932 to the spring of 1934. His leadership skills being recognized, Commander Stone served as the commanding officer for two vessels. The first was the Coast Guard Destroyer *Monaghan*, home-ported in New London, Connecticut, where he served as her commanding officer until June 1929. The second was the Coast Guard Destroyer *Cummings*, where he served until May 1931. Both destroyers were former navy warships that were turned over to the Coast Guard to help augment the fleet during the enforcement of Prohibition. He also served as the commanding officer of two air stations during his career, Air Station Cape May, New Jersey, and Air Station San Diego, California, as well as the senior member of several aviation boards and panels.

Elmer F. Stone was appointed a cadet in the Revenue Cutter Service on April 26, 1910. He qualified as a cadet after passing the required examinations, scoring higher than any other applicant that year. The first school of instruction to train officers in the Revenue Cutter Service was established on July 31, 1876, aboard the Revenue cutter *Dobbin*. Over the years, the school of instruction moved from the *Dobbin* to different training vessels, eventually moving to Fort Trumbull near New London, Connecticut, the year that Stone was appointed. Upon graduation on June 7, 1913, Stone was appointed as a third lieutenant in the Revenue Cutter Service.

TREASURY DEPARTMENT

OFFICE OF THE SECRETARY

WASHINGTON

April 26, 1910.

Mr. Elmer F. Stone,

#100 Redgate Ave.,

Norfolk, Va.

Sir:

By virtue of authority vested in me by the Act of Congress approved July 31, 1896, you are hereby appointed a Cadet in the Revenue Cutter Service of the United States to take effect from date of oath.

Respectfully,

Acting Secretary.

C. L.

H.

TREASURY DEPARTMENT

OFFICE OF THE SECRETARY

WASHINGTON

April 21, 1910.

Mr. Elmer F. Stone,

#100 Redgate Avenue,

Norfolk, Va.

Sir:

You are informed that you have passed the recent examination for cadet in the Revenue-Cutter Service, having obtained a general average of 85.61 per cent. Your standing was number one on the list of candidates.

Your appointment as a cadet in the Revenue-Cutter Service will be sent you in the near future.

Respectfully,

Captain Commandant.

The crew of the Curtiss NC-4 is shown shortly after arriving in Lisbon, Portugal: (from left to right) Chief Machinist's Mate Eugene S. Rhoads, U.S. Navy; Lt. James L. Breese, U.S. Navy; Lt. (jg) Walter Hinton, U.S. Navy; Lt. Elmer F. Stone, U.S. Coast Guard; and Lt. Comdr. A. C. Read, commanding officer, NC-4. Missing from the photograph is Ens. Herbert C. Rodd, USN. Stone received a written commendation from then Assistant Secretary of the Navy Franklin D. Roosevelt, dated August 23, 1919, that stated, "I wish to heartily commend you for your work as pilot of the Seaplane NC-4 during the recent trans-Atlantic flight expedition. The energy, efficiency, and courage shown by you contributed to the accomplishment of the first trans-Atlantic flight, which feat has brought honor to the American Navy and the entire American nation." On October 1, 1921, he was awarded the Victory Medal with Aviation Clasp, and on May 23, 1930, he was awarded a special Congressional Medal, especially designed for the occasion by the president in the name of congress for "extraordinary achievement in making the first successful trans-Atlantic flight."

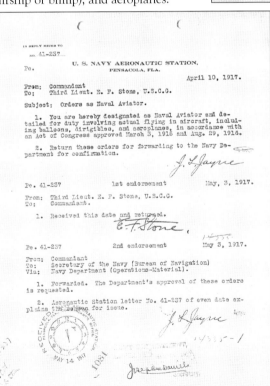

Upon completion of three years of sea duty, Stone requested assignment to aviation duty. On September 1, 1916, he was appointed a student aviator at Pensacola, Florida. After completing the course of instruction, then 3rd Lt. Elmer F. Stone was designated as a naval aviator on April 10, 1917, the first Coast Guardsman to do so. Since his winging, other Coast Guard members have been receiving their naval flight training in Pensacola along with members of the navy and Marine Corps. At that time, flight training lasted one year and designated him to fly any aircraft, "including balloons, dirigibles (airship or blimp), and aeroplanes."

Then Revenue Cutter cadet Elmer F. Stone (far right) was appointed as a cadet in the Revenue Cutter Service by the Treasury Department on April 26, 1910, at the age of 23. The School of Instruction of the Revenue Cutter Service, founded in 1876, would later go on to become the modern-day Coast Guard Academy located in New London, Connecticut.

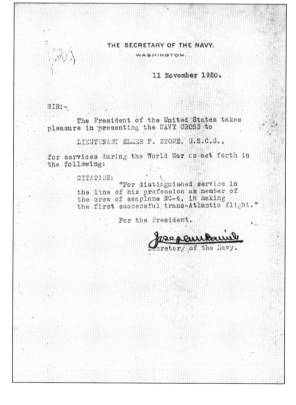

Stone was awarded the Navy Cross "for distinguished service in the line of his profession as member of the crew of seaplane NC-4, in making the first successful trans-Atlantic flight" on November 11, 1920. They were in direct competition with British pilots. All were hoping to win a prize of $50,000 offered by London's *Daily Mail* and awarded to the first team to successfully cross the Atlantic by air.

This photograph of the class of 1913 that graduated from the Revenue Cutter Course of Instruction was taken aboard the Revenue cutter *Itasca* in New London, Connecticut. Elmer F. Stone is in the front row, first on the left. Today's Coast Guard Academy graduating classes typically have between 150 and 200 new officers, quite the contrast to this early class of 16.

Elmer F. Stone was the first Coast Guard aviator and naval aviator No. 38 in the navy's roster of naval aviators. To date, there are around 3500 Coast Guard aviators. Bobby C. Wilks became the first African American Coast Guard aviator in 1957 (Coast Guard aviator No. 735). In 1977, Janna Lambine became the first female Coast Guard aviator (Coast Guard aviator No. 1812).

Form 2816 C
TREASURY DEPARTMENT
U. S. Coast Guard
Revised January 1936

REPORT ON THE FITNESS OF OFFICERS

Confidential

The following six questions are to be answered by the officer reported on:

Period covered by this report, from 1 October, 1935 to 20 May 1936 (1936).

STONE, Elmer Fowler ; Grade Commander ; U.S.C.G.
(Surname first - other names in full)

1. Regular station or duties Commanding Officer, Air Patrol Detachment, San Diego, Calif.
2. Additional duties performed
3. Permanent home address 3601 Lotus Drive, San Diego, Calif.
4. Next of kin Wife M.F. Stone 3601 Lotus Drive, San Diego, Cal.
   (Relationship)   (Name)   (Address)
5. (a) For what class of duty have you a preference? (if more than one, state order of preference)
   Aviation
   Sea
   (b) For what station have you a preference? (if more than one, state order of preference)
   San Diego
   New York.
6. Proficiency in foreign languages, stating which ones, and ability therein, giving mark:
   (a) As interpreter none
   (b) As translator none

   Signature E.F. Stone   Rank Commander, USCG

Following to be made out by Reporting Officer:

7. Reporting Officer: Name R.L. Jack , Rank Comdr. , U.S.C.G.
8. Reporting Officer's official status relative to officer reported on Section Comdr.
9. Assign marks on scale of 0-4 in appropriate subdivisions given below, and any other qualification on which observation has been sufficient to justify marking--a mark of 2.5 or less will be referred to the officer reported upon.

   Present assignment 4.0 . Ability to command 4.0 . As Executive or Division Officer
   As Deck Watch Officer In Administration 4.0

10. Has the work of this officer been reported on either in a commendatory way or adversely during the period of this report? If so, state the substance of the report. YES
11. In case any unfavorable entries have been made by you on this report, were the deficiencies indicated hereon brought to the attention of the officer concerned while under your command and prior to the rendition of this report? If yes, what improvement, if any, was noted? No Unfavorable Entries
12. Considering the possible requirements of the service in peace or war, indicate your attitude toward having this officer under your command. Would you---(1) Especially desire to have him? YES (2) Be satisfied to have him? (3) Prefer not to have him? (1) (3)---Refer to officer for statement.)
13. Has any weaknesses---mental, moral, physical, etc.--which adversely affect his efficiency? (If "Yes," give details.)

    No.

This is Comdr. Elmer F. Stone's officer final fitness report when he was the commanding officer of the air patrol detachment in San Diego, California. These reports, completed on an annual or semi-annual basis depending upon rank, assess and evaluate an officer's performance against officers of a similar pay grade. When evaluated for promotion or assignment to a specific job, a lot of weight is given to what these reports say. Commander Stone received excellent scores across the board, scoring well above average in every category. His strong points noted were leadership, loyalty, attention to duty, and presence of mind. Note the date of May 20, 1936, near the reviewing officer's signature. Stone's next evaluation was not due until May 31, but due to his death, the report was done early.

Crewmembers of the Curtiss NC4 are, from left to right, Lt. (jg) W. Hinton, U.S. Navy; Lt. Comdr. A. C. Read, U.S. Navy; and Lt. E. F. Stone, U.S. Coast Guard. Lieutenant Stone served as the navigator and a pilot during the flight and was the lone Coast Guard member among the navy crew. Serving with the navy was to become the norm for Stone throughout the 1920s.

The crews of the Curtiss NC4's with Secretary of the Navy Josephus Daniels and Assistant Secretary Franklin D. Roosevelt are shown on the steps of the Navy Department building upon their return to the United States. From left to right are (first row) Lt. Comdr. A. C. Read, Secretary J. Daniels, Comdr. J. H. Towers, Assistant Secretary F. D. Roosevelt, and Lt. Comdr. P. N. L. Bellinger.

This statue pictured today, and in 1949, was erected as a memorial to Comdr. Elmer F. Stone's service and now stands outside of the Sector San Diego Joint Harbor Operations Center. The citation that accompanies the memorial, dedicated on January 26, 1983, cites Commander Stone's accomplishments in pioneering Coast Guard aviation, specifically the use of aviation for search and rescue. Commander Stone's uncanny foresight and ability in aviation as well as his fine qualities of leadership made him respected and beloved by all who served under him. One officer who knew him well describes him as "pop-eyed, bushy-haired, stub-nosed, careless of dress but as alert as a terrier; a man who cared little for the form, but much for the matter."

The original air station search-and-rescue alarm was a brass bell that served the purpose of alarming the crews on duty of a search-and-rescue launch. The bell, which now stands in the center of the base near the flagpole, is engraved with the Coast Guard motto, *Semper Paratus*, which in Latin means "Always Ready." The origin of the motto "Always Ready" is not completely known. It is believed that, in the 1800s, the motto was associated with the then Revenue Cutter Service, referring to the fact that they were always under steam and always ready should they be needed. In 1927, when the official Coast Guard seal was officially authorized, the phrase was included surrounding the Coast Guard shield and thus became the official motto. Today the Coast Guard strives to maintain an "always ready" posture in carrying out a mission set that includes search and rescue, maritime law enforcement, aids to navigation, icebreaking, environmental protection, port security, and military readiness.

www.arcadiapublishing.com

Discover books about the town where you grew up, the cities where your friends and families live, the town where your parents met, or even that retirement spot you've been dreaming about. Our Web site provides history lovers with exclusive deals, advanced notification about new titles, e-mail alerts of author events, and much more.

MADE IN THE

Arcadia Publishing, the leading local history publisher in the United States, is committed to making history accessible and meaningful through publishing books that celebrate and preserve the heritage of America's people and places. Consistent with our mission to preserve history on a local level, this book was printed in South Carolina on American-made paper and manufactured entirely in the United States.

This book carries the accredited Forest Stewardship Council (FSC) label and is printed on 100 percent FSC-certified paper. Products carrying the FSC label are independently certified to assure consumers that they come from forests that are managed to meet the social, economic, and ecological needs of present and future generations.

FSC
Mixed Sources
Product group from well-managed
forests and other controlled sources

Cert no. SW-COC-001530
www.fsc.org
© 1996 Forest Stewardship Council

Find Your Place in History.